D1613651

DATE DUE

The 100th Day of School

JANUARY/FEBRUARY

by Melissa Abramovitz

Consulting Editor: Gail Saunders-Smith, PhD

CAPSTONE PRESS
a capstone imprint

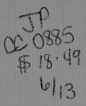

Pebble Plus is published by Capstone Press,
1710 Roe Crest Drive, North Mankato, Minnesota 56003.
www.capstonepub.com

Library of Congress Cataloging-in-Publication Data
Abramovitz, Melissa, 1954–
  The 100th day of school / by Melissa Abramovitz.
    p. cm. — (Pebble plus. let's celebrate)
  Includes index.
  Summary: "Full-color photographs and simple text provide a brief introduction to the 100th Day of School"—Provided
by publisher.
  ISBN 978-1-4296-8645-7 (library binding)
  ISBN 978-1-4296-9382-0 (paperback)
  ISBN 978-1-62065-304-3 (ebook PDF)
  1. Hundredth day of school—Juvenile literature. I. Title. II. Title: One hundredth day of school.

  LB3533.A37 2013
  394.26—dc23   2012003823

Editorial Credits
Jill Kalz, editor; Kyle Grenz, designer; Marcie Spence, media researcher; Kathy McColley, production specialist;
    Sarah Schuette, stylist; Marcy Morin, scheduler

Photo Credits
Capstone Studio: Karon Dubke, cover (boy), 1, 5, 7, 9, 11, 13, 15, 17, 19, 21, 22; Shutterstock: Christophe Testi, cover
    (jellybeans), Karen Roach, cover (pennies), 11

Note to Parents and Teachers

The Let's Celebrate series supports curriculum standards for social studies related to culture.
This book describes and illustrates the 100th Day of School celebration. The images support
early readers in understanding the text. The repetition of words and phrases helps early readers
learn new words. This book also introduces early readers to subject-specific vocabulary words,
which are defined in the Glossary section. Early readers may need assistance to read some
words and to use the Table of Contents, Glossary, Read More, Internet Sites, and Index sections
of the book.

Printed in the United States of America in North Mankato, Minnesota.

112012   007045R

Table of Contents

Hello, 100th Day of School! . . . 4

Adding Up to 100 10

Let's Celebrate! 16

Activity: A Learning Tree 22

Read More 23

Internet Sites 23

Glossary 24

Index 24

Hello, 100th Day of School!

Most celebrations happen on the same date each year. But the 100th day of school does not. Its date changes.

4

The 100th day of school comes in January or February. The date depends on when a school year starts.

Students and teachers count each day. On the 100th day, they celebrate the first 100 days of learning. All activities are about the number 100.

Adding Up to 100

You can count in many ways

to reach 100. Collect 100 buttons

or pennies. Group them

in piles of 5, 10, or 20.

Twenty piles of five equal 100. Ten piles of 10 equal 100. So do five piles of 20. How many piles of 2 make 100?

You can measure 100 in many ways. Measure how far you can walk in 100 seconds. Weigh 100 pieces of cereal and 100 pennies.

Let's Celebrate!

It's the 100th day of school!

How will you celebrate?

Jump 100 times.

Share 100 raisins.

Blow 100 bubbles.

17

Make a necklace
with 100 beads.
Do a 100-piece puzzle.
Connect 100 paper clips
to make a chain.

Help others.

Have your class donate

100 cans of food to a food bank.

Send 100 cards to thank

U.S. soldiers. Happy counting!

Activity: A Learning Tree

What have you learned in 100 days?
Make a learning tree to find out!

What You Need:

a large piece of tag board   scissors

a black marker   a glue stick

green construction paper

What You Do:

1. Draw a tree trunk and lots of tree branches on the piece of tag board.

2. Draw 100 leaves on the construction paper.

3. Write something you've learned on each leaf. Use classmates' names, books you've read, new words, or cool facts.

4. Cut out the leaves.

5. Glue the leaves on the branches.

Next year, start this activity on the first day of school.

Make one leaf each day for 100 school days.

Read More

Goldstone, Bruce. *100 Ways to Celebrate 100 Days.* New York: Henry Holt and Co., 2010.

Miller, Reagan. *100th Day of School.* Celebrations in My World. New York: Crabtree Pub. Co., 2010.

Schuette, Sarah L. *100th Day: A Spot It Challenge.* Spot It. North Mankato, Minn.: Capstone Press, 2012.

Internet Sites

FactHound offers a safe, fun way to find Internet sites related to this book. All of the sites on FactHound have been researched by our staff.

Here's all you do:

Visit *www.facthound.com*

Type in this code: 9781429686457

Super-cool stuff! Check out projects, games and lots more at **www.capstonekids.com**

Glossary

celebration—a special gathering

donate—to give something as a gift

food bank—a place for people in need to get food

soldier—a person who is in the military

Index

activities, 8, 10, 14, 16, 18, 20

counting, 8, 10, 12

dates, 4, 5

grouping, 10, 12

helping others, 20

learning, 8

measuring, 14

weighing, 14

Word Count: 196
Grade: 1
Early-Intervention Level: 16